About the Author

Cornwall is my homeland and as a Cornishman, by birth and ancestry, I am very proud of my Celtic and Cornish roots. I spent the first thirty years of my life on my family's farm, Little Skewes at St Wenn. I have travelled and there are many very beautiful places in the world, but there is nowhere else on the planet I could ever call 'home'. Crossing the Tamar back into Cornwall is always an emotional experience for me. I am a performance poet and despite having been registered blind for many years, I still perform my poetry under the banner of 'Clive Live'.

Clive's Uni-Verse

Clive Blake

Clive's Uni-Verse
A Cornishman's take on life

An A to Z
100 Poem
Galactic Tour

Olympia Publishers
London

www.olympiapublishers.com
OLYMPIA PAPERBACK EDITION

A CIP catalogue record for this title is
available from the British Library.

ISBN: 978-1-80074-334-2

First Published in 2022

Olympia Publishers
Tallis House
2 Tallis Street
London
EC4Y 0AB

Printed in Great Britain

Dedication

I would like to dedicate this book to my wife, Stephanie.
Without her patience, help and support, this collection
would not have been compiled.

Please note:

Although it is true that some have been captured, please be assured that no thoughts have been harmed during the making of this book. Also, these thoughts are organic, carbon-neutral and sourced from a sustainable mind!

Unfortunately, as regards allergies, we cannot guarantee that all of these poems have been produced in a nut-free environment!

[Credits]

Front cover image is of Showery Tor at night
Photography by Chris Robbins MPAGB, EFIAP
www.chrisrobbins.co.uk

Back cover image is of Clive Blake in 2021
Photography by Adrian Blake

Contents

FOREWORD

My poetry is, by nature, an eclectic mix of thought-provoking, reflective and humorous poems. The subject matter is diverse and totally random, ranging from abominable snowmen to escapee milk bottles, from land mines to zebras. It is the product of a totally chaotic mind!

Just like the Big Bang, which gave birth to our universe, it is completely random and chaotic in the initial explosion, but instantly coalesces into bigger and bigger clumps, eventually forming the planets, moons and all that now makes up our present universe. I'm confident that there is a semblance of order within this poetry collection somewhere; I just haven't managed to work out where, yet!

Please don't be put off by the randomness factor: if you embrace it, you might even find that you rather enjoy it!

A YOUNG CHILD'S SMILE

Countless millennia of the
Earth's molten core
Heaving on tectonic plates,
Have ripped continents apart
From gorge to sky,
The wonder is…
They can be bonded once again,
By a young child's smile,
In the mere glance of an eye.

ABOMINABLE SNOWMAN
AKA Sasquatch

The Abominable Snowman
May try to melt into obscurity,
Yeti remains a glittering star
On the ecological ladder,
After a very, very long climb.

Yes indeed:
Bigfoot is a leg-end
In its own time!

ALIVE AND WITH MEDALS

He stared at his war medals;
As bright as when first minted,
His own lustre long since tarnished;
Only tear-filled eyes now glinted!

He belonged to a generation
That sacrificed its fragile youth,
And traded it for our defence;
For freedom and for truth.

Although a very modest man
Who accepted his war-torn lot,
He wanted the world to remember,
All the others left to rot.

A past filled with campaigns like his,
Couldn't easily be put aside,
Though through many a tortured memory,
God only knew how he'd tried.

Don't ever forget this brave soldier,
Who now struggles to pull on his vest,
For if you forget the alive and with medals,
You'll surely, never remember the rest!

ALLOW ME THE TIME...

Allow me the time...
To stand and stare,
To ponder on the how and where,
To lose myself in thoughtfulness,
To unknot my mind's tangled mess,
To consider and to meditate,
To transform into a Zen-like state,
To notice reflections and reflect,
To self-diagnose and introspect,
To absorb all of nature's treasure,
And to enjoy this age-old pleasure,
Allowing my heart to beat more slowly,
Not thinking all creatures are below me,
To quietly try to comprehend,
The meaning of life and to what end,
To allow my soul to come into view,
To allow my spirit to mend, renew.

ANNIVERSARY OF A BLIND DATE

You could have called it a blind date,
The manner in which we first met,
But one that was truly desired,
Not one made for a stupid bet.

A year has now passed since that day,
My life then so completely changed,
When my future was realigned
And not just merely rearranged.

With the little sight I had left
I really liked what I first saw
But my social skills were lacking
And my emotions were red-raw.

She saw through my anxieties;
The pain I had coped with for years,
She seemed to sense the imprint left,
By many invisible tears.

Empathy was her strongest suit,
That was obvious right away,
Her bright sunny manner ensured,
We had an enjoyable day.

It's strange how two can so quickly
Be bonded and then become one,
And all seeming as natural
As the rising of the dawn sun.

With the little sight I had left,
I really liked what I first saw,
And I knew the feeling was mutual,
When she nuzzled me with her nose,
And then offered me her paw...

BLAME GAME

With a mentality as cold as an
Up high,
Sky spy,
Fly by,
Watch die,
Vulture…

I just cannot abide
This blame,
Then claim,
No shame,
Blame game,
Culture…

BORN TO

Born to search,
Born to seek,
Born to help,
The mild and meek.

Born to rule,
Born to lead,
Born to show,
We can be freed.

Born to Mary,
Born to atone,
Born to break
The hearts of stone.

Born to rally,
Born to rebel,
Born to dampen
The fires of hell.

Born to save,
Born to die,
Born a Saviour
For you and I.

BOTTLED DREAMS

Many, many years ago;
I put a message in a bottle,
And it floated far out to sea
To date no one has answered it…
But perhaps one day… one day…
One day… one day… maybe.

Many, many years ago;
I aspired to achieve a dream,
And my dream it lingers still,
To date I've not achieved it;
But perhaps one day… one day…
One day… one day… one day…
One day… I will.

BRIGHTLY FROM THE NIGHT SKY

Another star is twinkling now,
From the sky at night,
For your soul has flown to Heaven
And there it shines so bright.

You could not have been more loved
During your time on Earth,
For you caused so much happiness,
With your brand of love and mirth.

It is comforting to know that
Your love's still shining down,
So when we often think of you
It's with a smile and not a frown.

For life doesn't end; it's a circle,
Of that, I feel quite sure,
And one day we will join you and enter
That same revolving door.

BUMBLY BEES

I loves… I loves…
Bumbly Bees,
With skinny legs
And big fat knees.

With golden rings
And black ones too,
They buzzy buzz
As all bees do.

They hover low
As they have planned,
Choose a flower
And then they land.

Grabs some pollen
And buzzes away,
But will be back
One bumbly day.

I loves… I loves…
Bumbly Bees,
With skinny legs
And big fat knees.

BUT THIS IS AN EMERGENCY

Tell Dr Blood it's *Mrs Bloomsbury*;
He always sees *me* right away;
He's such a wonderful doctor — so much
Better than that Dr Day.

What the devil are you incinerating,
I consider your tone a right cheek,
I've not bothered you for ages; I've
Not phoned for at least... a week.

But this is an emergency;
Yes of course it's serious,
I'm sweating, shivering, sneezing
And feel quite delirious.

I'm running a terrible temperature,
I'm covered all over in spots,
My body aches from head to toe,
My muscles all tied up in knots.

My heart's got the palpitations,
Though I've still got a pulse — it's quite weak;
My poor throat's ever so red and sore,
It's increasingly hard... to... speak.

My eyes are all glazed and weepy,
My ears are infected and blocked,
I think there's a chill in my kidneys
And my joints have all stiffened and locked.

My stools — are alarmingly liquid,
My water's grey, misty and strong,
I'm suffering pins and needles, in fact...
I don't think I've got very long.

He can see me on Thursday morning,
An appointment for half past ten,
But that's no good at all to me...
I'll be better again by then!

CELEBRATING YOUR LOVE

We are here today to celebrate the love
You so obviously share,
A love you wish to formalise
And publicly declare.

A couple truly meant for each other,
A couple truly meant to be,
A couple whose friends and family,
We are very proud to be.

We hope your happiness continues,
That you have much more in store,
We hope the memories made today
Will stay with you — forever more.

CHARIOTS OF THE SURF

Surf's up.
Heads are down,
Timing their move,
Concentrated frown,
Salt lips,
Hard swallow,
Adrenalin pumping,
There is no tomorrow,
The white horses charge,
Their chariots follow,
Surfing speeding waves,
Above a spray-crested hollow,
For just a few seconds,
Taming the waves,
Anticipating the way
That nature behaves,
With triumphant abandon,
And balance supreme,
Living the moment,
Living the dream…

CHARLOTTE DYMOND

In early eighteen-forty-four,
In Cornwall's heart; on Bodmin Moor,
Charlotte Dymond, a young farm maid,
Had her throat slit with a steel blade,
She crossed fast streams and deadly bogs,
Found her way through mists and fogs,
But couldn't stop that fatal blow,
That stole her life and laid her low,
She walked to meet someone that day,
Just who that was… no one would say,
Found days later beside a track,
Laid on a cart; her shroud a sack,
The surgeon, Thomas Good, was fetched,
Had in his mind, her white face etched,
Charlotte untouched by fox or crow,
Had she been moved… he did not know,
No evidence was ever found,
But her young boyfriend had gone to ground,
Fingers so quick to point his way,
Matthew Weeks panicked; ran away,
The hapless cripple, was soon caught,
No other culprit was ever sought,
The judge was just a rubber   stamp,
Bodmin Gaol was dark and damp,
The scaffold built, the crowds arrived,
Matthew swore he had not lied,
The floor gave way, the rope drew tight,
Was justice done… the verdict, right?

CHRISTMAS FAMILY DINNER

"Is there anyone for stuffing?
Well done, George, send us down your plate,
Auntie, if you've finished with the cranberry sauce
Could you please pass it across to Kate?"

"Brian, can I interest you in my Brussels?
There's nothing quite like a good sprout,
If anyone wants anything passed,
Don't wait to be asked, just shout."

"Richard, will you please sit and eat,
And just stop irritating Claire,
No, you better wash your hands first,
You're getting gravy in her hair."

"Ted, you wanted more potatoes,
What, you only want one or two?
But the ones left really aren't that big,
I'd better pile on a few."

"Sarah, you're not looking after your young man,
The poor boy's been left to starve,
Go and get him some more turkey dear,
Your father will help you to carve."

"Malcolm, not too much in Grandma's glass,
You know what she gets like,
Open another red for Father,
I'll stick to the bubbly white."

"Well, if everybody's had enough,
I think I'd better finish the peas,
Richard, don't cough over the table,
Remember your manners, please."

"Ah, make way for Father and the Christmas pud,
I hope he hasn't overdone the brandy,
Saints preserve us… Father's on fire…!
Oh, well smothered dear, three cheers for Mandy,
Hip, hip, hooray,
Hip, hip, hooray,
Hip, hip, hooray."

"No, Louise, you can't pull the crackers yet,
We're saving those for tea,
Richard, take that stupid tinsel off your head,
And put it back on the tree."

"Everyone, go in the other room and play games,
Just leave all the dishes to me,
I'll do the washing and drying up,
While I'm sorting out something for tea."
"Richard, please don't tease the dog,
Claire, don't pin that tail on the cats,
Lloyd, play nicely, stop fighting with Louise,
You're ruckling up all of the mats."

"Hmmmnn… not quite enough sherry in this trifle,
Hick… I think there's probably more in me,
I'm sure I've been working far too hard,
Hick… I'm feeling quite dizzy."

"They say that Christmas comes but once a year
And aren't I just glad that's so,
It's nice to see all of them for a while,
But it's even better to see them go…"

CONFORM TO THE NORM

My baby:
Don't be too quiet, yet don't be too shrill,
Don't be too restless, but neither too still,
Please grow up hardy, yet soft to the touch,
Not seeking too little, nor asking too much.

Years later…
My child:
Don't be precocious, yet don't be too shy,
The middle-sized apple of your father's eye,
Don't be too forthright, nor keep to yourself,
Don't be too daring; but care for your health.

Years later…
My son:
Don't aim too high, nor get stuck in a hole,
Nor hang back if offered an uninspired role,
Please don't take the high road or even the low,
The main road is best… not too fast or too slow.

Years later…
My epitaph:
Here lies a man, who knew how to conform,
Who never left harbour, for fear of a storm,
Avoiding the hot and the cold for lukewarm,
In loving, but not too loving, memory,
Of your only son… Norm.

CORNISH EYE

I watched
A Cornish chough,
Flying so Cornish high,
Over Cornish cliffs,
In a Cornish sky,
All Cornish observations,
Made by my Cornish eye.

I watched
The Cornish sun,
Masked by a Cornish cloud,
I thought my Cornish thoughts,
My Cornish thoughts were loud,
I viewed the Cornish landscape,
And I felt so Cornish proud.

I watched
The Cornish waves,
Roll into the Cornish bay,
I saw the Cornish sunset,
At the end of another Cornish day,
For I am forever Cornish,
And forever Cornish I will stay…

CORNISH SHORE

The Cornish shore…
Where golden sand lies next
To dappled grey granite rock,
Where the sea breeze sweeps
And the mussels flock,
Where the rock pools gather
And the small crabs patrol,
Where the white foam curls
And the breakers roll,
Where the sea birds' call
And the salt spray stings,
Where the seaweed sunbathes
And the limpet clings,
Where a stream's course meanders,
And reflects the azure sky,
Where a starfish gazes skywards
And white clouds go scudding by.

By all means take treasured memories,
But please take nothing more,
And leave nothing but your footprints
On this sacred Cornish shore…

CORNISH TRADESMEN

Now, Cornish tradesmen do a proper job,
But they might not do it straight away,
For if they say they'll do it "dreckly",
There might be a slight delay…!

NB: Although the English "directly"
and the Cornish "dreckly"
sound very similar, they are poles
apart in terms of meaning!

CORNWALL EXPLORED

Coastline, rocky, rugged, proud,
Crumbling cliffs in ozone shroud,
Sun-kissed drifts of desert sand,
Golden frame of a sea-cradled land.

Fishing village, atmospheric hub,
Brass band playing, outside quaint old pub,
Boats, all sizes, rest near harbour wall,
Wading birds sift through tide-filled pool.

Foliage explosion of a Cornish hedge,
Country lanes snake, and young birds fledge,
Ruminants, punctuating, quilted hill,
Buzzards soar and wise hares are still.

Tin mine engine house, towering stack,
Roof caved in, gorse and bracken's back,
White clay peak, geometrical and sleek,
Earth's riches gouged, canyon deep.

Moorland, open, untamed, granite-strewn,
Wild ponies dance to a skylark's tune,
Tor and beacon, barrow and mound,
You're in God's own country,
When you walk this ground.

DANCE TILL YOU REACH THE MOON

Don't always march
To another's drumbeat,
Nor always dance
To another person's tune,
But march in time
To your own heartbeat and
Dance and dance,
Till you reach the moon...

DARKENED ROOM

Have you ever sat and pondered
In a darkened room;
Reality melting away
In the murky gloom,
Ignoring gravity's attempts
To try and hold you tight,
Heading off into space on a
Magic carpet flight?

Did you explore the Universe?
Travel through all time,
Contemplate your own existence;
Even think of mine?

Did you ever find the answer
To the question, *Why*?
Did you really want to return from
Flying through the sky?

Did you come back with a jolt when
Someone came in the room,
Did the bright light startle you;
Did reality resume?

DOES ANY

Does any fragile spring flower,
Not welcome the lengthening day?
Does any young wide-eyed puppy,
Need to be told when to play?

Does any green sapling not want,
To aspire to become a tree?
Does any blind person not dream,
That one day they'll wake and see?

Does any spider turn its back,
When its web vibrates with a fly?
Does any sleek eagle not wish to,
Claim mastery of the sky?

Does any wild cheetah refuse,
To chase dodging prey at full speed?
Does any farmer not work hard,
To ensure that his crops succeed?

Does any river not seek to
Meander its way to the sea?
Does any wild flower not wish,
To be pollinated by a bee?

Does any dry garden not wish,
To be moistened by morning dew?
Does any heart yearn more than mine,
To be loved forever by you?

DON'T LOOK BACK

Don't look back longingly,
To the youth that you once had,
You only remember the sunny bits,
Your mind has locked away all the bad.

Have your dreams and chase rainbows,
If that's what you want to do,
But enjoy the present, and look to the future…
For that's all that is waiting for you.

EBB AND FLOW

The seasons come,
And the seasons go,
The seasons ebb,
And the seasons flow.

The spring green hue,
The rich autumn gold,
The clear summer blue,
The grey winter cold.

The changing mask
Of our Mother Earth,
Winter her death,
And spring her rebirth.

Spring starts the tune,
Autumn beats the time,
Summer sings the song,
Winter blows the chime.

The seasons change,
Yet all stay the same,
Nature's illusion;
Her own magic game.

The seasons come,
And the seasons go,
The seasons ebb,
And the seasons flow…

EXTENSIVELY TATTOOED

Do you ever wonder
How you would be viewed,
If you became extensively —
Extensively tattooed?

Would you be transformed
Into a real cool dude,
If you became extensively —
Extensively tattooed?

Would your partner join you,
Or would the suggestion be pooh-poohed,
If you became extensively —
Extensively tattooed?

Would you bare all,
But not feel nude,
If you became extensively —
Extensively tattooed?

Do you think the artwork
Could help lift your mood,
If you became extensively —
Extensively tattooed?

Do you think it would change
My critical attitude,
If I too became extensively —
Extensively tattooed?

FALL LIKE A FEATHER

You must fall like a feather
And bounce like a ball,
If people cut you short
You must stand really tall.

If kicked while you're down
Make sure that you get up,
Show you're a dog with teeth
If they whip you like a pup.

If they dampen your spirit
Show your hope is still dry,
If clouds cover your parade
Make your fly-past extra high.

If hit hard below the belt
Smile and shake their hand,
If your life goes off course
Just imagine it was planned.

Flex and bend like a willow
But retain a heart of oak,
If someone upsets you
Try and treat it as a joke.

You must fall like a feather
And bounce like a ball,
And — always come out fighting
When your back's against the wall.

FIRMLY ANCHORED

You are my heartbeat's echo,
My spare rib, who's guilt free,
You are an essential part,
The half that completes me.

I'm sure there is no universe
Where more love I would find,
But should an offer come my way
It'll gladly be declined.

I seek no other harbour,
I'm as happy as can be,
And I'd only ever sail away
If you were there with me.

FREEDOM

Don't try to end my liberty,
Don't try and cage me in,
Don't try and control my thoughts,
Free thinking is not a sin,
Don't tell me who I can mix with,
These choices are mine alone,
Don't invade my privacy,
My private life is my own,
Don't stop freedom of expression,
Don't stop freedom of speech,
Don't rewrite or cancel our history,
But instead, open-mindedness teach,
Millions of people have died for it,
For freedom's worth fighting for,
So it's crucial to protect freedom,
For it's too late…
When it exists no more!

GAZEBOS

Millions used to roam across Africa's plains,
But, sadly, not one gazebo still remains,
Yes, unfortunately, they are now extinct,
Their fate and Man's greed, clearly linked.

Treasured for their waterproofed hides,
Used as marquees by jetsetters and blushing brides,
Eyelets used to mask inappropriate holes,
Their thin straight legs used as supporting poles.

The world's appetite for awnings was immense,
Pressure on their survival became too in-tents,
Most were poached — but some were boiled,
Corruption rife and palms were oiled.

Did I detect tears in Attenborough's eyes,
As his films captured the gazebo's sad demise?
Let the whole world learn from this,
Not allow species to head into an abyss,
Never let us again, our powers abuse,
Just so we can enjoy shaded barbeques!

GLEAMING WHITE MERINGUE

Gleaming white meringue,
What made me buy it?
It's not part of my diet,
I'm inclined to bite it,
But I'm trying to fight it!

My conscience's view of it:
Sugary,
Sticky,
Synthetic,
Sickly.

My stomach's view of it:
Scrumptious,
Salivating,
Seductive,
Sense pulsing.

Actually:
It's Inanimate,
It's Inconsequential,
Its Inanity
Is Innate.

In…
Ate…
TOO…
LATE…

GREEN CAR

A rover you were, all your working life,
But your conscience caught up with you,
You chose honourable re-tyre-ment and
You're now *green* through and through.

Once you greedily thirsted for petrol,
But finally kicked the habit,
And you now partake of fresh country air,
Just as rural as any wild rabbit.

In the past your throaty engine's roar
Out-decibeled the traffic's bustle,
But you now much prefer to listen to
The dry, restless leaves which rustle.

Alas your coachwork no longer gleams,
But you still retain all of your pride,
It's just your wish to be *at one* with nature,
As everything else you've tried.

A frosty morning is no deterrent,
To a well-seasoned convert like you,
It's just an unavoidable prelude,
To the sparkling spring-time dew.

Your days of *road rage* long since gone,
When you used to speed and scramble,
You're now content to pull to one side,
And be overtaken... by a bramble.

HARVEST MOUSE

Oh, little mouse,
You are so small,
You are petite,
You are so cute,
You are so sweet.

With grasping tail
And tiny feet
You climb tall stems
Of swaying wheat.
Reaching the top
You eat the grain,
Then skilfully,
Climb down again.

Oh, little mouse,
You are so small,
You are petite,
You are so cute,
You are so sweet.

HER YOUNG EYES

Her young eyes…
Gazed into the darkness,
Gazed into the night,
Gazed into the distance
Which was…
Far, far, far, from sight.

Her young eyes…
Gazed away from the present,
Gazed away from the past,
Gazed towards the future,
Which was coming to greet her…
Far, far, far, too fast…

HOPE

When you are at your lowest ebb
And you are feeling really low,
When you are on the edge of an abyss
And can see nowhere else to go,
When life's treatment of you seems unfair,
When the odds seem stacked against you,
When you want to improve your situation
But no improvement comes in view,
When you seem to have dug a hole for yourself
But somehow can't stop digging,
When your ship's mast has crashed to the deck
And you're tangled in the rigging,
When you only flourish in the light
But the dark is closing in,
When you crave a fair share of the cake
But your slice is cut too thin,
When you fight hard and fight again
But no battle you ever win,
Then there is only one thing that keeps you going
And only one thing that helps you to cope,
It's the thing humanity treasures most of all,
It's a little thing called… hope!

I AM THE NIGHT SKY

You are the viola,
And I am your bow,
You are the mountains,
And I am your snow.
I am the song sheet,
And you are my tune,
I am the night sky,
And you are my moon.

You are my true love,
The love of my life,
My best friend, my lover,
My soul mate, my wife.

I LOVE YOU MORE THAN YESTERDAY

I love you more than yesterday,
And less than I shall tomorrow,
You are the path to my happiness,
An antidote to any sorrow,
When I think I can't love you more,
I find I can, and indeed, I do,
But the most amazing thing of all is,
You say the same is true for you...

I ONCE HAD A RELATION-SHIP

I once had a relation-ship,
But she sailed far away,
Up-anchored and set course to find
Another sheltered bay.

Our stormy and tempestuous affair
Had ended, sunk at last,
The current which pulled us apart,
Had run so strong and fast.

She didn't even wave, but left me
At low ebb, high tide,
Her face was stern, my head was bowed…
My salty tears to hide.

My flag, alas, she flies no longer
From her stately mast,
Our swell affair was present tense,
But sadly now 'tis past.

She left full speed ahead, her sails
A'billowing like a cloud,
If happiness equals silence,
My heartbreak's cannons loud!

I stare from port, my eye on a star,
Bored, like a boat without rudder,
My emotions beached on a lonely shore,
Left to flounder and shudder.

A vessel like her will shore-ly land
Another love-struck fool,
I'm only one fish in a big, big sea...
And her heart is fathoms cool!

IF YOU COULD SHRINK INFINITY

If you could shrink infinity,
And then place it inside —
Just one grain of sand,
My love for you would
Fill the universe,
And would still be —
Desperate to expand.

ILLUSION

Although Mother Nature
Has been raped and abused,
Her basic laws ignored,
So misread and confused,
Our living world remains
A most beautiful place,
A jewel that stands out
From the darkness of space,
Help her to recover;
Nurse her back to full health,
For without her, how empty…
The illusion of wealth.

I'M FEELING INSPIRED

My heart's pumping,
My brain's starting gun has fired,
Watching Stephen Hawking on TV
Has made me feel inspired.

He's working out the laws of the Universe,
The mysteries of creation to unravel,
I still haven't fully grasped the rules
Of either Monopoly or Scrabble.

He agrees that the Universe is made from string,
As the Super String Theory suggests,
Whilst I thought string was only good
For making fishing nets and vests.

He's trying to work out what happened
Fourteen billion years in the cosmological past,
I can't even work out what happened to myself,
The Friday before last.

He's mathematically calculating what happens
On the edge of a Black Hole,
I'm mathematically struggling with additions,
And my seven times table.

Despite my lack of brain power, I'm inspired
To challenge Stephen Hawking's theoretical Big Bang,
Surely if the Universe is made of Super String,
It would have been more of a Big Twang?

IN CARDBOARD BOXES

People living in cardboard boxes...
What are they doing there,
Are they there out of choice,
Or there in despair?

Are they there through their own fault,
Or is the blame society's at large,
Should you give them some free assistance,
Or have police put them on a charge?

Unlike the Good Samaritan,
You choose to walk on the other side,
Quite happy to debate lofty moral issues,
Until you meet reality, stumble and collide.

Cardboard City's inhabitants,
Are surely past redemption,
Would you really make that statement,
If in there, lived your son?

Shouldn't they help themselves more?
Perhaps they've already been trying,
All I know is they are fellow human beings,
And in the winter... they are dying.

IN THE QUIET OF THE NIGHT

In the quiet of the night,
Where darkness steals the need for sight,
When most are asleep, I lie awake,
Waiting for the dawn to break,
Long past trying to count sheep,
My brain's shallow, but my thoughts are deep,
My mind's trying to put the world to rights,
But I think it might take… several nights!

IT CERTAINLY WOULD

When the wisest man in the world said
"It would be a tragic shame if ever
The Great Forest were to be reduced
To a small clump of trees."
Everyone, without exception, answered
"It certainly would."

So when The Great Forest
Was eventually reduced
To a small clump of trees,
That is what they decided to call it…
It Certainly Wood.

I'VE FOUND SOMEONE WHO...

I've found someone who…
I can love forever — I love so much,
Their loving ways, their caring touch,
Will stand by me when times are tough,
Never saying that they've had enough.

I've found someone who…
Can raise my smile and decrease my frown,
Will help me up when I'm feeling down,
Will make life's worries melt away,
Providing the sunshine of my day.

I've found someone who…
Will always listen, try to understand,
Will guide me with a patient hand,
Will love me both in body and soul,
Making my happiness their main goal.

I've found someone who…
Will be both gentle and be kind,
No better soul mate could I find,
Always willing to talk things out,
Never needing to rage or shout.

I've found someone who…
Is willing with me — to share their life,
To make us a team of man and wife,
But most of all — I've found a friend,
Here by my side — till my life's end…

JUSTIFIED

A teenage pessimist lived,
With a fear and a dread,
That one day he'd awake,
And find himself dead,
He lived his life under,
This cloud and this gloom,
Lived a reclusive existence,
In a dark windowless room,
Others thought he was strange,
But his fears were justified,
For he had premonitions and dreams,
In which he had indeed died,
Then one day he became so,
Very seriously ill
His fever too strong to be cured,
By a mere potion or pill,
At Death's door he struggled to cling on,
To the things that he knew,
But his doctor somehow managed,
To help pull him through,
So his predictions and fears,
Had indeed now come true,
For he had sadly died at the age,
Of one hundred and two.

KINDNESS

If everyone had enough social blindness to ignore
Gender, disability, religion and race,
This world would be a much,
Much, much, better place.

If everyone in this world showed kindness
To everyone else that they met,
Then reaching Utopia on this planet,
Would be a — pretty safe bet.

LET ME SAIL AWAY FOREVER

Let me sail away forever,
Let me cast off from the shore,
Let the swirling mists engulf me,
Till reality rules no more,
Let me sail the mighty oceans,
Let me pass by cliffs anew,
Let me navigate a passage
Through the rolling veil of blue,
Let my anchor never hold me,
Let my sails always billow out,
Let me sail away forever, and
May I never turn about.

LICHEN LADEN GRANITE CROSS

Lichen laden, granite cross,
Reminder of a Celtic culture's loss,
An icon to placate a harsh deity,
A religious symbol, an outward plea.

Laden cross, granite lichen,
Not a mere whim, but a deliberate decision,
Ley-line power, here to focus,
Awaiting another mid-summer solstice.

Granite cross, lichen laden,
Sculptured for a dark-haired maiden,
Elaborate and ultimate statement of love,
A prayer for a union to be blessed from above.

Cross, lichen laden, granite
Manufactured on a far-off planet,
Crafted and left to become immortal,
Marker of a time traveller's portal.

MARRIAGE BLESSING

We know your wish to unite
Is so truly meant,
Let your love be the stone,
This blessing — the cement.

May you build on firm foundations,
And never build on sand,
May you both embrace the future,
And approach it, hand in hand.

May your love for one another
Increase with each new day,
Bringing you true happiness,
Never causing you dismay.

May this blessing merely be
The very start of your new life,
May your dreams become reality,
Now that you are man and wife.

MY D FENCE

There's a fence all around me,
It keeps people away,
It gives me space of my own,
It keeps others at bay,
I constructed it myself,
It's the price I must pay.

It goes up for a mile,
While still touching the ground,
People have searched for a way in,
But one has never been found,
It's an impenetrable barrier,
That no sledgehammer can pound.

Does it make me feel claustrophobic,
Or does it make me feel secure,
Once I knew all the answers,
But now I'm not so sure,
Shall I make a hole in my fence,
Shall I fill it with a door?

Here I am stuck
In a defensive retreat,
I once so craved victories,
But I feared more a defeat,
Should I tunnel under my fence,
Should I dig really deep?

Should I stay here in my cocoon,
Or should I go out and explore,
Should I try again to embrace life,
Even though I failed once before,
Shall I cut a hole in my fence,
Need I bother fill it with a door?

My fence was to keep others out,
But it is both friend and foe,
For it also keeps me in,
When all I want is to go,
Shall I place explosives around it
And wait for it to blow?

All right you win, I'm coming out,
Waving a white flag up high,
I hope I fare better this time,
'Cos I'm reaching for the sky,
I'm taking off my lead boots,
This time... please help me to fly!

MY PRAYER

Dear Lord,
Don't let me ask only for myself,
For problems solved and better health,
Nor ask only for kin and friends,
With minor ills and moral trends,
But make me think in global terms,
Where drought kills and injustice burns,
Please tend to their greater needs first,
Help heal their wounds and quench their thirst,
My patient faith can wait till then,
My prayer sent —
Goodnight —
Amen.

NO MALICE SHOWN

See the owl in swift silent flight,
Surfing the darkness of the night,
In control of its black domain,
Its prey killed quick, no time for pain.

Don't be outraged when its victim dies;
The owl's not a mugger of the skies,
No malice shown when it hunts for meat,
It leaves alone what it cannot eat!

NUFF SAID

Besotted,
Beloved,
Be brave,
Betrothed,
Be wed.

Be kind,
Be loving,
Be faithful,
Be happy,
Nuff said.

OBLIVION

Mankind seems oblivious
To Nature's pleading cries,
Mankind seems oblivious
When Nature ups and dies,
Mankind seems oblivious
To its carcass filled with flies,
Mankind seems oblivious
To God's wrath above the skies.

Man can only think of seeking treasure,
Man can only think of funding leisure,
Man can only think of his own pleasure.

Oblivious to Nature's sighing,
Oblivious to Nature's crying,
Oblivious to Nature's dying…

OLD WRECK-MARKER FROM FOWEY

(Fowey is pronounced Foy, as in boy.)

There was an old wreck-marker from Fowey,
Who had been at sea since he was a buoy,
But when his mooring wore through,
He went where the wind blew,
Ending his days on the beach — as a toy.

ONE DAY I DREAMED

One day I dreamed…
There was no longer any 'Third World',
Just a united 'First',
Famine clearly vanquished forever,
And no one died of thirst.

Power was never used to enslave,
And wars were fought no more,
Man's resources were pooled together,
To help aid all the poor.

Man respected his fellow creatures,
Living in harmony,
The oceans free from all pollution;
Helped by 'green' energy.

People didn't need to live in fear;
Crime a thing of the past,
A planet no longer fragmented;
A one-peace world at last.

I awoke in time to catch the news;
News of crime, famine, war,
Moist-eyed I headed back to my bed,
To try and dream… some more!

OSTRI-SIZED

People call me ugly,
And other hurtful names,
I'm often ostri-sized,
My feathers used for games.

They say the *Ugly Duckling*
Grew up to be a swan,
And though I'm still but very young,
They ask me, *What went wrong?*
I'm left here on my ownsome;
And feel so sad and blue,
Well, you would feel the same
If you were an... emu.

OUR FUTURE QUESTIONED

One night...
I thought I'd glimpsed the future,
In a nightmarish scene,
Where lives were sad and pointless
And life was simply mean,
Where people feared the future
And craved the world's past,
Where people wanted answers
And then these questions asked:
"Where are all the insects?
Where are all the birds?
Where are all the fish and
Where are all the herds?"
Sadly, there were no answers,
Sadly, there were no words...

OUR JOURNEY

We embark on a new journey,
Let our travels never end,
Keep us heading in the same direction,
Though the track may sometimes bend,
Let happiness be our destination,
Let our trademark be a smile,
Let us enjoy every footstep,
Not begrudge a single mile,
Let us revel in new discoveries,
Greet each fresh dawn with pleasure,
Let us find our inner wealth and know...
The true meaning of treasure.

PL-EASE

Don't see only our disabilit-ease,
Don't deny us basic facilit-ease,
Don't ignore our many abilit-ease,
Don't compound our varied difficult-ease,
Deal head on with the harsh realit-ease.

You never know what life has in store,
You may fall one day and rise no more,
You may join our ranks, afraid, unsure,
You may write words to plead; implore.

We are not an alien race,
We have a voice, we have a face,
We have our part to play; a place.

Let us join life's lively dance,
Let us have an equal chance.

Pl-ease.

PLEASE DON'T TRY AND PUSH ME

Please don't try and push me,
Don't hustle and crowd me in,
I need some space to find myself,
To work out where I fit in.

Please don't try and push me,
Just let me go at my own pace,
As the tortoise proved to the hare,
There's more than one way to win a race.

Please don't try and push me,
Don't assume that you know best,
Although we all look much the same,
I am very different from the rest.

Please don't try and push me,
Just let me go at my own speed,
I know where I want to go in life
And I'm sure I will succeed.

PRAY FOR THEM

The muggers,
The rapists,
The murderers,
The paedophiles,
The confidence tricksters —
Pray for them.

The weak,
The naïve,
The young,
The old,
The inadequate mixers —
Prey… for them.

QUALITY TIME

I want to walk in my golden years,
On the Cornish beaches' warm gold sands,
Where my footsteps are unhurried,
And my route is seldom planned.

I want to sit on the wooden benches,
Overlooking those dark blue bays,
I want to breathe in this fresh salt air,
Until the ending of my days.

I don't want to become immortal;
Living for forever and a day,
I just want to savour life in this world,
No matter how long or short my stay.

I don't want my life extended for the sake of it,
With no reason or rhyme,
I just want to live in the here and the now,
And enjoy this — my quality time.

RAINDROPS DESCEND

Raindrops descend, puddles form,
A stream engulfed, a river is born,
A course is set, the sea to reach,
Meandering ponderously to a far-off beach.

The sea reclaims its myriad young,
Kidnapped by clouds, thunder-slung;
The storm is long past with calm all around;
Albatross glide, with a whisper of sound.

Seagulls circle, dogfish sleep,
Gannets dive and dolphins leap,
But black clouds return and lightning flashes
O'er storm-tossed seas, as thunder crashes.

Once more a stealthy cloud abducts infant water,
The sea's own offspring: a son… a daughter;
The thief sets off at a wind-blown pace,
The anguished mother unable to chase.

The criminal finds refuge in a partisan crowd,
A formless body in a vaporous shroud;
The cloud has no guilt, shows no remorse,
But heads inland on a predestined course.

A hill stands guard, like a customs post;
It stabs the guilty, but allows past the host;
The rogue cloud is ruptured, severed seam and pleat,
Releasing its captives and accepting defeat.

Raindrops descend, puddles form,
A stream engulfed, a river is born,
A course is set, the sea to reach,
Meandering ponderously to a far-off beach...

RE: COILS

What a great reptile,
A *Royal Python* — no less,
A serpent so dapper;
Never seen in a mess,
Non-poisonous, deaf, mute;
Except for its hiss,
It likes nothing more
Than to hug and to kiss!

Though it has no arms,
Harmless it is not,
Make no mis-snake a
Mean streak it has got,
Outside of its coils
The view is just fine,
But if invited inside
You'd be wise to decline!

Don't be enticed in
By its hypnotic stare,
For when those coils tense,
They act like a snare,
For those patterned coils;
Look brill from without,
But lose their appeal
When wrapped around
Your snout!

REQUIRED NO MORE

Do you know what it's like
To be required no more,
To be put out to grass,
To be kicked out the door,
To know your work's ended,
No more will be done,
To be slung on the tip,
Pushed aside by the young,
To be pensioned off
In an unceremonious way,
To know you've had yours,
Every dog has its day,
To have an appetite for work,
But be left to hunger,
To be replaced by someone
Less able but younger,
To be told you're too old,
When you feel in your prime,
To be sent on your bike,
Before it's your time,
To be all washed up
And flushed down the drain,
To have no physical wounds,
But still be in pain,

To feel your age,
Find you're no Peter Pan,
To see your life going
No longer to plan,
To recall when you felt rich,
But now you feel poor,
To hear your heart slowly pumping,
Alas it races no more,
To experience an emptiness
That nothing will fill,
To have no medical symptoms,
But still feel ill,
To be out of control
Of your own destiny,
To be constantly asking
Why me… why me?

REQUIRED ONCE MORE

Do you know what it's like
To have your freedom back at last,
To be able to choose new colours
Once pinned out of reach to the mast,
To find tho' you've lost your employment,
You can still retain all of your pride,
To discover the grass is greener
On the unexplored other side,
To patch up your battered ego,
Once thought irretrievably torn,
To feel a strong urge to celebrate,
When others expect you to mourn,
To take a fresh look at careers,
When you thought it was all in the past,
To discover your destiny's liquid,
And never in concrete cast,
To realise your aspirations,
Which no more are held on ice,
To alter your life's ingredients,
And add a small pinch of spice,
To discover you're no longer frightened
By things that are different or new,
To embrace all those sensible changes,
And take a much loftier view,

To keep everything in context,
And never let monsters appear,
To look to your dreams and take aim,
Keeping your sights crystal clear,
To be intimidated no longer
By applicants younger than you,
To know a wise captain will always
Choose an experienced crew,
To retain your sense of adventure,
Your instinctive love of fun,
To put down the now closed chapter,
And enjoy the one just begun,
To be welcomed back to life's table,
And invited to sit down and dine,
To feast till you're utterly bloated,
And swill it all down with sweet wine.

RESTING IN PEACE

Life's hustle and bustle has ended,
Now I've passed away, deceased,
My new terra firma home,
A guarantee of eternal peace;
Never disturbed by clamour or noise,
I don't even hear a sound,
In this world unknown to the living,
Within the ravenous ground,
No one here is the least impressed
By status, rank or class,
Deep below the skylit realms
Of fresh green, new-mown grass,
The worms treat everyone the same,
Whether noble born or serf,
As I idle away my leisure hours,
Under neatly replaced turf,
No need ever to work again,
I've had my share of toil,
As my weary bones I rest forever,
Amidst the once feared soil,
I reflect on life's rich journey,
A long winding path, well-trod,
Time for contemplation assured,
Beneath the mounded sod,
This place is now home to me,
I don't think of it as a tomb,
Birth and death entwined as one,
In Mother Nature's womb.

SAVE OUR PLANET

Ban the bomb!
Save the whale!
Please don't step on
That poor snail.

Help the ozone;
Retain your wind,
Don't use aerosols;
They should be binned.

Pesticides are bad,
Composting's good,
And only use soft
Sustainable wood.

Leave forests alone,
Stop 'slash and burn',
From our past mistakes…
Can't we all learn?

Save endangered species,
Give them some space,
Help them compete
In an unequal race.

Recycle your waste,
Throw nothing away,
It'll come in useful
One fine rainy day.

Single-use plastic
Is clogging the seas,
We must all change our ways
For our planet's sake — please.

SET IN STONE

My love for you will never end,
Will never break, will never bend,
Will not tarnish or grow weak,
No love but yours I wish to seek.

It will not fade or disappear,
It will not stray, or even veer,
My love for you won't change or alter,
My heart is true, won't stumble, falter.

My love for you
Is set in stone,
For this ring is for you
And for you alone…

SMOKING GUN

Who ruined my confidence,
Who trampled my young dreams,
Who turned the signpost around,
Who undid all my schemes?

Who was responsible,
Who held the smoking gun,
My parents, my teachers, my friends,
Could I afford to trust anyone?

Who deterred me from trying,
Who played on my self-doubt,
Who kept me on the outside,
Who locked my brave heart out?

I looked all around me…
Accused everyone,
But no one would admit to holding…
The smoking gun!

Who helped make me a loner,
Who turned well-wishers away,
Who spawned paranoia,
Who kept loved ones at bay?

I glanced in the mirror,
When a glance wasn't planned,
To see with disbelieving eyes,
The smoking gun… in my hand!

THAT LIFE WAS MINE

That life was born in Africa,
In a poor, dusty, rural part,
His parents had few possessions,
He only desired their heart.

That life fought hard against disease,
Which time after time, nearly won;
His parents' love saved him, urged him to fight,
Just as they had done.

That life suffered terrible hunger and thirst,
As famine and drought were neighbours;
He worked with his parents whilst very young,
Undaunted by childhood labours.

That life lived through civil wars; he lost
Two cousins and one best friend;
The hatred he could not understand,
He prayed for the fighting to end.

That life gained an education, determined
To try to break the mould;
The treasure he knew could be found within,
Not panned for, like fool's gold!

That life then studied medicine,
A doctor's arduous training,
Wanting to bring relief and care
To all the poor there, still remaining.

That life stepped onto a landmine...

THE AGE OF INNOCENCE

The age of innocence,
A daughter we adore,
Long hot summer days,
A toddler, only four.

Tadpoles in a jam jar,
Watching as they wriggle,
Nature being studied,
Inviting her to giggle.

Eyes filled with laughter,
No clouds hide the sun,
Happiness a toddler's gift,
Enjoyed by everyone.

Wide-eyed and innocent,
To her, life's one big game,
If only we could join her...
Be innocent, once again.

THE BATTLE RAGED

The battle raged,
The arrows flew,
We were brave, but
We were few.

Out numbered,
Out fought,
Out flanked,
Out thought.

An arrow sought,
An arrow found,
I took the brunt,
I hit the ground.

In animate,
In pain,
In jured,
In vain.

Soldiers rarely say die,
Soldiers rarely grow old,
But my body grows weak,
But my body grows cold.

Ex pired,
Ex haled,
Ex tinct,
Ex... *failed*...

THE GHOST OF CHARLOTTE DYMOND

Charlotte died in eighteen-forty-four,
Murdered on Cornwall's,
On Cornwall's, Bodmin Moor,
Those seeing the ghost are very sure,
It's poor Charlotte,
Poor Charlotte, who still walks the moor.

A monument erected is there to this day,
Marking the spot,
The spot, where she did last lay.
Those seeing the ghost are very sure,
It's poor Charlotte,
Poor Charlotte, who still walks the moor.

Was it her murderer the police did arrest?
But if so, why can't her spirit,
Her spirit, now find its rest?
For those seeing the ghost are very sure,
It's poor Charlotte,
Poor Charlotte, who still walks the moor…

THE INVINCIBLE BIRTHDAY CANDLE

"The Greatest… the Most Superb…
The Invincible Birthday Candle…!"
It was at the peak of its career,
It was much too hot to handle.

Its boasts always waxed, never waned,
It made the other candles sick,
Its bragging claims enough to get on
A more modest candle's wick.

No challenger came forward…
Though not through lack of spine,
They just watched and waited,
Preferring to bide their time…

Night after night, it would bluster away:
"On me, no other candle is a patch,"
Then one day it was stuck into a cake,
And it finally met its match.

THE LIGHT

A Light so brilliant;
It can break the blackest dark asunder,
A Light so powerful;
It can outstrike lightning in full thunder,
A Light so glorious;
It can fill all who see it with wonder.

And...
Although so very bright;
Its rays will never blind,
Although always present;
It is not easy to find,
Although it is so mighty;
It is gentle as can be,
And if anyone were to follow it,
It would show them... Eternity.

THE SLEEPY OLD OWL

The sleepy old owl
Watched the waterfowl,
As some moorhens floated by.

The ducking ducks dived
Where the cute coots thrived,
The fox looking on from the dry.

The sleepy old owl
Watched the fowl as well,
As more moorhens floated by.

The dragonflies flapped
Where the greedy pike snapped,
A heron looked down from on high.

The sleepy old owl
Watched the ripples swell,
As even more moorhens floated by.

Then a mournful song
From a lonesome swan,
Caused all to take to the sky.

The sleepy old owl
Then took off as well,
And no more moorhens floated by…

THROUGH THE HOLE IN THE GLASS

Behind an old window,
A young girl often gazed,
Through a thin shattered pane,
Through a large hole unglazed.

Wistfully observing
The uncaring world pass,
Feeling invisible
To the more wealthy mass.

When life became too tough,
Her daydreams would unfold,
As protection against her
Brave hopes growing cold.

Where her mind could explore,
Expanding like light-gas,
And her thoughts could escape
Through the hole in the glass.

TINY HANDS

Tiny hands and tiny feet,
You're so very small and neat,
Your little life, now just begun,
Our hearts you have already won,
Your lovely newborn baby smell,
We are truly under your spell.

Tiny feet and tiny hands,
You are the centre of our plans,
You look so perfect lying there,
We cannot help but gaze and stare,
You look so peaceful when asleep,
You have made our dreams complete.

TOAD IN THE HOLE

Though I'm ugly and I'm old,
And I'm fat and I'm bald,
And I'm grey and I'm cold;
I've still a story to be told…

I've never been a handsome prince
As far as I can tell;
Unless I lost my memory
During a witch's evil spell!

I started my spawned life in a pond,
In that valley, there beyond,
I haven't always been a toad-in-the-hole,
I was once, a cute tadpole,
Hmmmn… those were the days.

I'm a source of fear for superstitious folk
The hapless butt of many a joke,
I'm not endearing, or the least bit cute,
With all the charm of a hobnail boot.

I'm not a worshipper of the sun,
My warty skin preferring it dank,
So I make my home in a shaded hole,
In a man-made stone hedge, or a bank.
You might think that I'm between
A rock and a hard place,

That I've got my back to the wall,
But it's me that's never worked,
Paid tax or had a mortgage,
And never had to go to school!

TOMORROW NEVER COMES

It's true, tomorrow never comes;
In the last seconds of the day,
When darkness reigns
And moonbeams play,
When tomorrow's late approach
So inevitably nears,
It's today, not tomorrow,
That so freshly reappears.

TRAPPED

Do you feel like a trapped spider
In an upturned glass?
Do these feelings come and go,
Do you think that they might pass?
Have your insecurities and doubts
Expanded into fears?
Have these anxieties deepened
And increased in recent years?

Well...
You need much more self-belief,
Your courage you must amass,
For the cure is in your own hands,
Only you can break the glass...

TWO HUNGRY LITTLE PENGUINS

Two hungry little penguins
Both eager for their nosh,
One penguin's name is Splish,
And the other one's called Splosh.

Two hungry little penguins
Each holding out their dish,
I wonder what's for dinner?
Surprise, surprise — *it's fish.*

UNCLE ALBERT

He was always known to everyone as Uncle Albert,
He used to sign all my birthday cards as Uncle Albert,
He used to turn around when I shouted Uncle Albert,
He was who we visited when we went to see Uncle
Albert.

But I'm sorry to say, he's now belated,
Sadly passed away, dead and cremated.

And what I can't understand,
And what I am eager to learn,
Is why has everyone stopped calling him Uncle Albert,
And started calling him Uncle Ern?

VOID

Don't go near a vacuum,
Stay clear of empty space,
Don't look at the dark side,
But watch the full moon's face.

Don't fall into a pit,
Or get stuck in a hole,
Avoid incompleteness,
Learn to worship the whole.

Don't slip into a chasm,
Place your footsteps with care,
And always make sure that
You're spatially aware.

Nothingness is harmful,
Keep barren thoughts at bay,
Harness your potential,
And you will win the day.

Let your thoughts be wholesome,
Thinking much less like Freud,
But most of all remember to —
Avoid a void…

WE CORNISH ARE A NATION

Cornwall is almost an island,
Thanks to the River Tamar and the sea,
Its indigenous inhabitants are us Cornish and
We Cornish are a nation — and will always be.

Kernow (Cornwall)
Boasts its own:
Parliament and laws homegrown,
Flag, anthem and crest with fifteen bezants,
Cornish pasty and "Oggy Oggy" chants,
Patron saint and noble kings,
National bird with its black chough wings,
Unifying tagline of "One And All",
Cornish wrestling and silver hurling ball,
Ethnic minority status, unique DNA,
Cornish language still spoken today,
Nationhood recognised worldwide,
Facts are facts and the facts can't hide.

We embrace our British neighbours
And we respect the Queen,
But we Cornish are a Nation
And we have always been.

Westminster chooses to ignore this fact,
Let it relent and admit its shame,
For whilst the truth beats in Cornish hearts,
A nation — we shall remain...

WEDDING VOWS

May we forever be lovers,
May we forever be friends,
And should we hurt each other,
May we quickly make amends.

May we enjoy our passion,
But never let compassion die,
Thinking in selfless terms as *we*,
Never emphasising *I*.

May we forever be soul mates,
May our love eternally last,
May the food of love sustain us,
May we never have to fast.

May we use each other's strengths,
When we are feeling weak,
May we both learn to compromise,
And always as one voice speak.

May we never keep dark secrets,
May we never tell each other lies,
May we both work unceasingly,
To ensure our love never dies.

WHEN MY MUM WAS VERY TALL

Many, many years ago,
When my mum was very tall,
When I wasn't very old;
Before I had started school.

The sun was always shining,
And buildings were much bigger,
I used to drive a dumper truck,
And I filled it with my digger.

I shot the cowboy baddies
Who threatened me with danger,
My six-shooters both asmokin';
For I was the Lone Ranger.

Under the large oak table,
Or up in the apple tree,
I used to make secret camps,
But my dog would always find me!

Though the days were very long,
Bedtime always came too soon,
I'd sometimes get all drowsy,
And be carried to my room.

My pine bed was very large,
But still no room for my head,
Till I rearranged my friends;
And then moved along Big Ted!

I'd love to go back once more,
And play under clear blue skies,
Explore a world of wonder…
See again with wide young eyes!

WHO IS DISABLED?

Who is disabled?
Is it me, or is it you?
Should disability be based
On an anatomical stocktake,
Or based on what you can do?

For I can climb mountains,
I can soar through the sky,
And I can slay dragons,
With just a blink of an eye,
I can overcome barriers,
Fight against impossible odds,
Ignore patronising glances
And condescending nods.

So who is disabled?
Is it me, or is it you?
It is completely subjective,
It's just your point of view...

WHO IS THAT STRANGE OLD MAN?

I'm staring at this old man,
The old man's staring back,
His eyes are dull and misty,
His skin is weathered and slack,

Most of his teeth are missing,
And his cheeks are all caved in,
He has tufts of fluffy grey stuff,
Where the hair on his head had once been.

Who is that strange old man,
And why, oh why, does he stare,
Where on earth has he come from,
And how did he get over there?

He has the neck of a vulture,
His shoulders are feeble and round,
Decades of gravity have bent him,
Till his head is close to the ground,

His ears are as thin as paper,
His veins are showing through,
His nostrils are like forests where all
His hair has migrated to,

His body is skeleton-thin,
His ribs are all open-plan,
There's something rather pathetic,
About this strange old man.

His stare is quite unnerving,
It fixes me to the spot,
As if he remembers something,
Which I have certainly not,

He surely can't have anything
At all to do with me,
He looks well over ninety…
And I feel like twenty-three.

Suddenly a voice comes from nowhere…
"Come on Dad, you old fool,
You've been ages in the bathroom,
And I've got to get to school!"

Oh drat my failing memory,
How fuddle-headed can I be?
That old man staring from the mirror…
Why of course — *now* I remember — it's *me*!

WISDOM IN TRIPLICATE

Heading into Bethlehem…
Three Wise Men,
In search of a stable.

Heading out of Bethlehem…
Three Wise Turkeys,
While they were — still able.

WORDS CAN

Words can implore, words can plead,
Words can fail, but also succeed,
Words can empower, when at their best,
Can help to clear, what is on your chest,
Words can soar and words can plunge,
Words can embrace and words can lunge,
Words can hurt and words can kill,
But words of peace are stronger still,
Words can be shallow, words can be deep,
Words can even help, you to get to sleep,
Words can inspire you, or invite you to dream,
Can take you to places, where you've never been,
Words can start wars, that they cannot easily stop,
Can cause West End plays to succeed, or even to flop,
Words can be helpful, give you direction in life,
Can help secure a union, between man and wife,
Words can be spoken quickly, or maybe slow,
Like a river's rhythmic and ever-changing flow,
The truth can be spoken, but so can a lie,
Words can enlighten you, or perhaps just mystify,
Words can confuse, words can even scheme,
Simple words may not be what, at first they might seem,
It is words, not dogs, that are Man's best friend,
For they will remain faithful until, the bitter end,
For words can inform and words can impress,
Sometimes much more can be said, with a lot less,
Words can capture your heart, make you feel free,

When put in the right order, they can form poetry,
Words can summon angels, or be devil-may-care,
Words can come singly, or joined as a pair,
Words can embellish, words can belittle,
Words are robust and supple, not weak or brittle,
Words can be cruel and words can be kind,
They need your guidance, for all words are blind,
Words can be thrown away, or treasured for life,
Can be as soft as a pillow, or as sharp as a knife,
Words can be shouted in public, or whispered while alone,
They can be forever silent, on paper and stone,
Words can be invented, words can be brand new,
Words can conflasculate... which they often do!

X MARKS THE SPOT

X marks the spot
Where a young child had stood,
Enjoying his friends' company as only
A young child could.

X marks the spot
Where the child lay dying,
Medics there to save his life,
Desperately trying.

X marks the spot,
From which the crowd was kept,
The child's mother who broke through
And uncontrollably wept.

X marks the spot
Where the ambulance came,
The police taking measurements,
Photographing the stain.

X marks the spot
Where the piles of flowers were left,
Where the moving tributes were made
From those now bereft.

X marks the spot
Where the funeral procession slowed,
Where a community's grief
In rivers now flowed.

X marks the spot
Where the young child was struck
By a man on a mobile
In charge of a truck.

X marks the spot
Where a quick call was made,
The cost of this phone call
Extravagantly paid.

YE KNOW NOT WHEN

Tick-tock and then chime;
Our life-clock beats
Our precious time out,
As it slowly depletes.

No one can know when
Their own clock will stop,
Will it end on a tick
Or will it end on a tock?

Each hour on the dot
Our clocks clearly chime,
To remind us all
Of our passing time.

Use your time wisely,
For ye know not when,
As engraved on the sundial;
On the church at St Wenn.

YIG AND YOG

There were two bottles of milk
Their names Yig and Yog,
Who planned a daring escape
In the early morning fog.

Forced to become cereal killers,
The mere thought made their white blood curdle,
As they struggled to free themselves
From their plastic milk crate girdle.

Yig said to Yog:
"If you make it to the newspapers,
Tell 'em everything that's passed-your-eyes,
How the TV adverts with the happy bottles
Are all just propaganda — lies."

They managed to wriggle free of the crate,
And they then jumped off the float,
Even though the other bottles s-creamed:
"No…! be careful…! Don't!"

They hit the road with an awful smash, and
Then rolled out of control in the dirt,
The next day… the news headlines read:
YIG DEAD and YOG HURT.

YOU'LL KNOW

No mathematical formula
Can define love on a page,
No statistician can measure it,
There exists no such gauge.

Love cannot be ordered,
Nor can it be planned,
Not pulled out of a hat
By deft sleight of hand,
Impossible to touch,
But it can be felt,
It is best when it's shared,
But it can't be dealt,
Invisible to all;
Gives no peacock show,
Has no shape, size or form,
But yes — it can grow.

In spite of this —
When you're in love, be assured...
You'll know... you'll know.

YOU'RE NEVER TOO OLD

You're never too old to learn something new,
You're never too old to explore,
You're never too old to have hopes and dreams,
You're never too old to want more,
You're never too old to make a difference,
You're never too old to aim higher,
You're never too old to change the world,
You're never too old to inspire,
You're never too old to share your thoughts,
You're never too old to give,
But mostly, people must realise…
You're never too old to live.

ZEBRA

The zebra:
An optical illusion
That tricks your sight,
Not colour, not HD ready,
But just in black and white.

An African sales success,
Of great pride it's the source,
Cleverly marketed as…
A barcoded horse.

BACKWORD

If you have enjoyed this book, please tell everyone about it. If you have NOT enjoyed this book, please keep it to yourself. Why should you be the only one to suffer?

Poetry Projects:

My main artistic collaboration, over many years, has been with my good friend and brilliant Cornish photographer, Chris Robbins. A collaboration which gave birth to our book "View Points and Points of View: A 'Phoetry Book' from Cornwall", a fully illustrated colour hardback, which was first published in 2009.

I have since also collaborated with other photographers and artists. Many of my poems can be found on the internet. My poetry has, over the years, found its way onto CD, DVD, apps and videos and into hardback, paperback and e-book.